A MAD LOOK AT THE 60's

Written by
NICK MEGLIN

Illustrated by
GEORGE WOODBRIDGE

Editorial Consultant
Diane M. Korn

WARNER BOOKS

A Warner Communications Company

Dedicated to:

noun n. the name of a person *(i.e. Dave Wedeck),*
place *(i.e. Stuyvesant High School),*
or thing *(i.e. tennis racket)*

. . . three wonderful nouns that have
contributed much to my life . . .

n.m.

WARNER BOOKS EDITION

**Title "MAD" used with permission of its owner,
E.C. Publications, Inc.**

This Warner Books Edition is published by
arrangement with E.C. Publications, Inc.

**Warner Books, Inc.
666 Fifth Avenue
New York, N.Y. 10103**

Ⓦ A Warner Communications Company

Printed in the United States of America

First Printing: April, 1989

10 9 8 7 6 5 4 3 2 1

ATTENTION SCHOOLS

WARNER books are available at quantity discounts with bulk
purchase for educational use. For information, please write to:
SPECIAL SALES DEPARTMENT, WARNER BOOKS, 666 FIFTH
AVENUE, NEW YORK, NY 10103.

CONTENTS

The nation maintained its interest in

SPORTS

in the 60's, only the preferences changed. As a spectator sport, baseball had lost its "national pastime" ranking. Football took over the country...

...and with that takeover, of course, came the old formula:

Success + Popularity = Big Bucks

Many college stars switched to business and accounting majors to keep up with the new version of the good ol' school spirit—

SIS! BOOM! BANK!

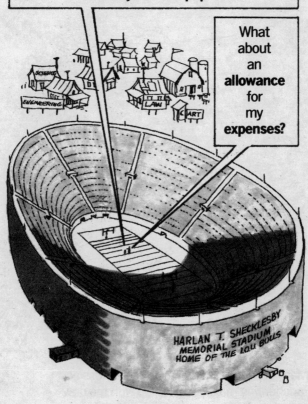

Listen, can I borrow someone's helmet for just one play? I'm gettin' a bad headache from the way their right guard is beltin' me on every play!
My ankle's gone! Maybe the coach will substitute somebody from off the bench!
What bench? And what somebody? Only 10 of us showed up to play as it is!
13

Hey! Why's this huddle taking so long? Won't we get penalized for "delay of game"?
Nah, they gotta retrieve the ball from the stands after the last field goal attempt! Besides, the officials have no clock! So how can they call "delay of game"?
9
15

Football, of course, made its ascent at the expense of baseball! Loss of interest meant loss of revenue, and baseball owners tried desperately to come up with gimmicks and promotions to lift sagging gate receipts. One of the more popular ideas was "give-away days" at the ballparks...

Hey, Mom, look! Today was **"Bat Day"** at the stadium!

Tennis, on the other hand, attracted many new fanatic followers eager to participate in a game that combined the physical skills of sports with the emotional skills of business! It provided endless opportunities for strategy and cheating, interwoven in a network of confrontation designed to delight sadists and masochists alike!

In the 60's, over 95% of the tennis rackets in use were made of wood, but many manufacturers, aware of the "tennis boom," experimented with metals and other materials. Old school hackers argued that metal rackets would eliminate the "feel" that wood rackets offer when destroying one out of frustration and disgust…

Considered more the game for the genteel than the slob, court etiquette can disguise the latter to appear the former. For instance, it is always polite to say, "Good game," to your opponents after you've smashed, slammed, and lied your way to victory all afternoon! "Nice shot," is what you say after you flub any ball hit to you! The shot itself can be a soft, ineffectual, easy put-away, but if you slop it up you can cover up your obvious inadequacies by acting as if the ball was more difficult to handle than it appeared! The same rule applies to receiving serve—anything you can't return is a "Great serve!"

Strategy is of prime importance to the game of tennis, and the novice becomes an easy victim to the well-seasoned practitioner until he develops counter-strategies of his own. For example, playing with one's own can of balls is stupid and unnecessary. By imitating the approach of a restaurant pro who times his reach for the check within a split-second after someone else picks it up, you too can appear ready to open a new can of balls just as the gust of air escaping from another's can signals the "all-clear" alarm…

One strategy absolutely essential for those dedicated to winning is opponent intimidation. One technique which has proven very successful is to let the racket fly out of one's grasp early in the game. The opposing player's concentration will be centered more on the racket than the ball, an obvious advantage to the "flinger" over the "duckee"...

The main strategy in playing doubles involves choosing a strong partner. If that cannot be achieved, at least each team member can blame the other for losing the match rather than having to bear the responsibility themself…

Just as the margin of victory is sometimes measured by a few lucky hits (or mis-hits), the strategy of timely "bad Calls" can also make that difference. A standard rule to follow is:
WHEN IN DOUBT, CALL IT "OUT!"

Tennis lessons fall into two main categories—"con job" and "for real." *Con job*—The tennis pro suggests you get "screened" by one of his assistants to judge the present level of your game. If you are a woman, you get somebody like Lance Scorewell...

Here, try holding the racket this way...

Oh, that feels better.

I thought it would.

How long do we keep practicing this grip?

It depends on you...

I'm a slow learner!

If you are a man, you get somebody like Chrissy Buttmaster…

Should you be unfortunate enough to hook up with a tennis establishment that may actually attempt to improve your game, your tennis pro will most likely be on the order of Mark De Sade...

Okay, you inept swine, racket back, bend those ugly knees, and hit through the @#$%&* ball like you got a muscle in that limp wrist!

The lesson to be learned here is that sometimes being conned can be a lot more fun than trying to improve your ability at some silly game!

LIFESTYLES

came in many, well, styles of life. For instance, there was an important segment of the population who, at first glance, appeared to be just like everyone else—plain, normal-looking folk. They weren't! If you studied some of their habits or funny ways at parties...

...or maybe the strange way they walked down the street together...

...you'd know in a minute these pour souls suffered from a new way of life that swept the country... **TRAILER LIVING**

ADVANTAGES OF TRAILER LIVING

Trailers provided all the necessities of a non–mobile home, as the following floor plan will attest. It should be noted that this is the floor plan of a trailer standing perfectly still...

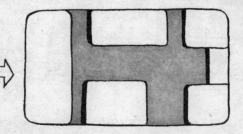

Some variations were observable when the trailer went up or down a hill or made a sharp turn...

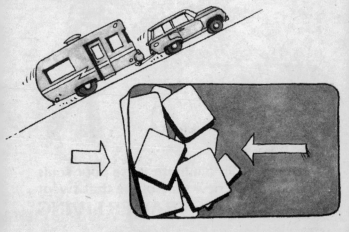

Small foreign cars did experience some difficulty dragging heavy trailers up a steep hill...

...but that balanced out with how easily heavy trailers dragged small foreign cars down the hill!

Magazines, catering the the mobile lifestyle, offered tips for trailer living...

On the road, no trailer owners lost sleep because of noisy milk men and garbage collectors, since none ever came...

They had no broken toasters or washing machines to contend with since they had no electricity...

They had no loud, nerve-wracking traffic jams to put up with since they weren't permitted on major roads and highways...

They read no horrible news or gossip since they couldn't be reached by phone...

As a trailer owner in the 60's, you were not alone. There were thousands of trailers on the road...

...and thousands more off the road, either in ditches or the bottom of ravines! But those were the brakes!

I want to take this opportunity to thank the **publisher** for making it **possible** for me to appear in this book, and my **policeman's salary** for making it **necessary!** This **"guest appearance"** is known as **"moonlighting,"** a common practice in the 60's that enabled people to improve their lifestyle. Although the term was coined to describe **cops** who worked second jobs, it soon became the accepted description for **anyone** involved in a "second income" venture, whether performed **subtley** "by the **light** of the **moon**" or in **obvious,** broad daylight...

You are one **lucky guy** since I got here just in time to **save your life,** fella! **Next time** you **may not** be so **lucky!** And you wanna be sure that if you're **not,** God forbid, you can at least make those you **leave behind** a little lucky, **right?** Well, this **"Disaster Delight" insurance policy** that I've got right here will do the job! They'll be **dancing** on your **grave,** believe me! You gotta **pen** on you?

In the 60's, the word "family" took on new meanings and different forms...

...but however different, some "families" held on to their traditional values...

There are **families** and there are **Families,** Salvatore! You gotta learn the **difference** or you can get yourself in **big trouble!** And how do you become a **member** of the **Family?** The **old-fashioned way**—you **earn it!** By **actions,** by **deeds,** by **contracts,** by **favors!** Today is a **solemn occasion!** You must **honor** the **father** of your bride by showing proper **respect** with a proper **gift!** You must **shoot someone!**
Today?

Listen, let's not make such a big thing of **who!** It's **expected!** The victim will **understand!** But don't pick some **bum** off the streets! My friends will **laugh** at me **behind my back!** How about the **Best Man!**
My cousin Frank? Please, Don Veto, not **Frank? We grew up** together! How about **Ralphie,** one of the **ushers?**

You **understand,** Salvatore? You want **fun?** There's **plenty** of women out there for **that! Not my daughter!** That's why **tonight,** after the wedding, she comes **home** with **us** while **you** go on the **honeymoon! Understand?**
Yes, Don Veto...
FRANKIE GEE'S "MUSICA DE SICILIA" BAND

Title songs gained eminence in the

MOVIES

of the 60's, and their themes were often more intelligent, better written, and more entertaining than some of the "flicks" themselves.

A "musical score card" of the decade's films include popular hits like...

JAMES BOND

Bond, James Bond—they call you;
Double-O Seven—they call you;
Whatever the time, wherever the place—they call you;
When "M" tells you there's trouble—you gotta go—
Whether to break the bubble of Dr. No,
Or shave the stubble off Blofeld's head
Right now, Mr. Bond, please get out of bed!
As for Pussy Galore and Dom Perignon, there's no time to refill...
Just be sure to pack your gun and your license to kill!
'Cause Oddjob may try to stall you!
Rosa Klebb may try to maul you!
Domino may Thunderball you!
But don't linger with the lass;
No, don't pour another glass,
Or you may find a Goldfinger in your Aston-Martin!
Yes, the one souped-up by "Q"
To be driven just by you—
To perform those crazy stunts on snow and ice!
So you won't die even once...though you only live twice,
Through each push and shove
Sent from Russia with love!
So please go, Double-O—you're getting us nervous!
You've wined and dined, now we're in a bind,
So bear in mind that you're still assigned
On Her Majesty's Secret Service!

THE GRADUATE

You've been in a coma
Since you got your diploma,
My son, the graduate;
Now the time has finally come
To show the world you're not a bum—
My son, the graduate!

We have a girl for you, she's like no other;
If you play your cards right,
You can see her at night;
In the day you can stay with her mother!

Because you see, my son, the graduate
I don't care if all your schooling has found
That too much fooling around
Can make you a total spastic!
So you're a physical mess,
You can still find success
My son, the graduate—in "Plastic"!

PSYCHO

Oh, a boy's best friend is said to be his mother;
With Norman Bates this certainly holds true;
Mum may wander for a spell
Off her rocker, raising hell—
Otherwise it's hard to separate the two!

Norm and mummy own a motel off the highway,
And should a guest show up to rent a room,
Mum might grab a knife and shriek
(She's quite a "cut-up," so to speak),
Then Norm cleans up the mess with mop and broom!

So in case some lonely night their place you're passing,
Just drop in on Norman and his mother...
You will be surprised to find
They're so similarly inclined—
You can hardly tell the one nut from the other!

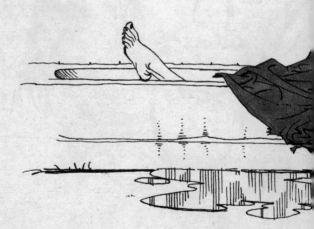

BONNIE and CLYDE

What kind of game are you playin', Bonnie and Clyde?
A game can be fun
If a game can be won,
But there's no winnin' and there's no thanks
For silly pranks like robbin' banks;
You're certain to come to no good
When you're merely a misunderstood
Robbin' hood!
This ain't Sherwood Forest, Clyde!
From this Sheriff you can't hide!
Bonnie sure ain't no Maid Marion;
And though she's as deadly as the gun she's carryin'
Those ain't merry men with a bow and arrow;
So goodbye, Bonnie Parker! Adios, Clyde Barrow!

THE HUSTLER

Will you wind up behind the eight ball, Fast Eddie
From pushing your cue stick too far?
You'll always make bucks
From gullible schmucks—
So why not stay right where you are?
Just follow the hustler's Golden Rule—
"Don't let 'em know there's a shark in the pool!"
There's a sucker born every minute
With cash, and you know you can win it!
Without worry or risk you're filling your quota
So why play the Fat One who's from Minnesota?
But in case you do choose to play with an equal
Should you—God forbid—lose…
Better pray for a sequel!

EASY RIDER

Loving you isn't easy, rider!
The things you do are pretty sleezy, rider—
Like picking up drugs across the river
From the lowest of thugs who pay to deliver
Their garbage up here—that's the way you're employed;
You don't give a damn for the lives you've destroyed!
So let's get down to the nitty-gritty:
Why are you expecting pity?
'Cause some good ol' boy has fired his gun?
Didja ever think that maybe his son
Was also shot-up, but not with lead?
He's alive, but as good as dead!
Drugs or bullets—what's the dif?
Either way you end up stiff!
No, loving you isn't easy, rider!
You've redefined the word "sleezy," rider!
What you've sown you now reap,
And the world's a better place without you, creep!

MIDNIGHT COWBO

I've found me a home
Where the perverts all roam,
Where the wild and the wacky all play;
Where the weird and the bearded,
The shaved and depraved,
The bugged and the drugged,
The morbid and sordid—
And Ratso and me can have our way
With the straight and the bi and the gay;
Yes, I've found a new home
Where the perverts all roam—
And right here in Times Square I will stay!

LOVE STORY

Love means never having to say you're surly—
Though you've always been rather obnoxious, girlie!
With your snide remarks and zingers that cut
There were times I'd like to have kicked your...
But...I couldn't do that, even though I was mad.
After all, I am a Harvard lad

And not some slow, low-brow male,
The likes of which you find at Yale,
With their brains in their...
But...there's no use denying
The fact that you're dying—·
Why waste time with lying?
So start your "Good bye-ing"
And stop with the crying!
Remember, my dear,
We must not shed a tear;
It's not part of the plan
For a Radcliffe girl or a Harvard man;

For, as is so often said,
If you're gonna be dead,
It's best to go quickly,
Not hang around sickly;
So let your put-downs finally cease, and then
Your foul mouth, love, will rest in peace! Amen!
Yes, you're dying for sure, my dear Jenny,
'Cause as far as a cure, there ain't any!
So many have died from what you've got—
A case of "Terminal Hollywood Plot"!

In the corporate world of the 60's, it was

BUSINESS

as usual—a simple matter of dollars vs. sense! Image was what it was all about, be it corporate or individual, and if the "unwritten rules" were written, it might look something like…

The BUCK STARTS HERE

A Handbook for
Business without Ethics

CREDO I   It is not what you do, it's how you do it!

Public Relations people created our **image!**

Market research supplied us with our **approach!**

Headhunters have secured the highest caliber team of executives and management available!

CREDO III Don't waste time finding reasons for failure —it's a lot faster and easier finding scapegoats!

CREDO V Creativity can always transform negative to positive, minus to plus.

Gentlemen, I'm sure you've all heard that we're in **serious trouble!** While our line of television sets was **acceptable** by **government standards, consumer standards,** unfortunately, are **much higher!** The public **didn't buy!** However, we **still** stand to make **huge profits!** Our research men have come up with a **viable solution!** You're on Kroul...

Business, of course, couldn't exist without some level or form of

ADVERTISING

and promotional considerations, for as one pioneer of that industry proclaimed, "A product isn't a product until people know it exists, it can't sell until enough people believe it's worth buying, and the advertising profession can't make it unless enough people believe this whole crock!" And so the art of selling became a science, the science of selling became an art, and if the "unwritten rules" that govern Madison Avenue were ever published, it might look something like...

CREDO I Sex can sell anything! If the commercial is sexy enough, the mind will not focus on the need for the product!

CREDO II Get someone with the right stuff to endorse your product. You can get a lot of mileage for a product by utilizing the reputation of certain celebrities despite product and reputation being totally unrelated.

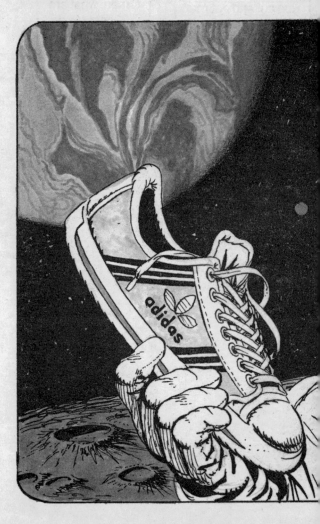

CREDO III Even a modest claim, when well-placed, can be more effective than an exaggerated claim.

CREDO IV Creative packaging will force them to buy more than they need!

Gentlemen, in the **past**, if you wanted **one tomato** for a salad, you'd **buy one tomato!** With **multi-packing**, you have to buy **6 at a time**, 2 of which are green and the other 3 over-ripe to go along with the **one tomato** you wanted to begin with!

LAW AND ORDER

Under the judiciary laws of this country, a person is innocent until proven guilty. If not proven guilty, he walks out free. If proven guilty, he can still walk out free if the plea is "insanity"!

The JUDGE: There are two basic standards for this politically appointed position. ONE, if the person's record as an attorney indicates this person cannot hack it practicing law, and TWO, if the politician appointing this person owes this person a favor.

The JURY: This body is selected from U.S. citizens who either cannot find meaningful employment, or those who aren't creative enough to invent reasons or excuses for avoiding jury duty. Once selected, the jury must decide which lawyer was the more entertaining and award that person the victory. Sometimes a jury spends many hours in deliberation before they decide what they want for lunch.

BUILT BY
AFTERTHOUGHT
CONST. CO. INC.
CONTRACT # 23758

LAWYERS: A lawyer's job is to find some flaw in some ancient edict so that his guilty client can be proven "innocent."

Eureka! This is it! Albanese vs. Fiore! A **dissolved partnership!** Albanese claimed ownership of the firm's season baseball tickets! Fiore claims they should go to **him** and runs down Albanese with his car on a sidewalk in Yonkers, injuring his leg! Judge Maligno, an ardent **baseball fan,** rules in **favor** of Fiore, citing "gross abuse and criminal negligence with intent to provoke and mentally incapacitate" on the part of Albanese! Fiore not only gets off **scott free,** he gets the **season's tickets** as well! Now, if I can show due cause that **my client,** a resident of Brooklyn and former Brooklyn Dodger fan, suffered "mental cruelty and personality abuse" before he tried to **strangle** this sun-baked Californian, Los Angeles Dodger fan swine...

Lawyers often try to set their fees on a "contingency" basis.

With doctors showing the way to make even bigger bucks than before, lawyers soon followed suit (after suit) as specialists! "Expand your fee by limiting your practice" soon became the modus operandi that ended the days when a person went to a local, neighborhood lawyer for legal assistance...

This was a time when legal and moral obligations to contracts and agreements were constantly being questioned and challenged. The courtroom had definitely been a battleground for entertainers, athletes, and large corporations, but now neighbors, small business people, and even friends and relatives began to put it in writing...

BINDING CONTRACT BETWEEN MOTHER AND SON

*Let it be known that I, _____
mother of the unappreciative (and spoiled rotten)
_____, agree to CEASE and DESIST*

1. *Nagging ("Reminding" someone what they should be doing is "nagging"?)*
2. *Treating him like a baby (even though he acts like one!)*
3. *Calling him "Ta-ta-la." (He should know what I'd really like to call him!)*
4. *Calling his shlemiel friends "shlemiels." (You call "garbage" garbage, right? You don't call garbage "gold," do you?)*
5. *Pressuring him about schoolwork. (Insisting on straight 'A's" so he can be a doctor is "pressuring"? In my time this was called "guidance." Go know with kids today!)*

PROVIDING SAID SON SHOULD:

1. Pick up his own clothes from all over the house (I don't have enough to do?)
2. Stand up straight and not slump over (like his spineless father).
3. Eat everything on his plate that I sweated over a stove all day to make. (There are people starving in the world today that would better appreciate my cooking, believe you me!)
4. At least apply to medical school now (Even though he's only 14 and just starting high school—why wait until the last minute? Am I wrong for being sensible?)
5. Promise to marry a nice, sensible girl who knows how important it is for a son to call his mother every day. (Not like the airhead from Santa Monica his older brother married!)

Now really, am I asking too much?

(Signed) _____
                                  (Mother)

           _____
                                   (Son)

BINDING CONTRACT BETWEEN TELEVISION REPAIRMAN AND OWNER

I, the undersigned repairman, agree to service the T.V. set belonging to you, the undersigned owner, and thereby restore order and harmony to your disrupted home PROVIDING I hear not so much as a <u>whimper</u> when:

1. *My actual bill exceeds estimate by $100.*
2. *My promise of repair within "two days" becomes "two weeks."*
3. *The set breaks down within one week after repair.*
4. *You get great reception only when you stand next to the set and hold antenna in your hand.*

_____   _____
      (Owner)   *(TV Repairman)*

LIVING AGREEMENT BETWEEN WIFE AND SPORTS-NUT HUSBAND

I, _____, agree to never again disturb my husband, _____ while he is watching any sport or sports related program. (Heretofore, "sports" will be defined as anything from pre-season baseball to championship frisbee tournaments, including halftime nonsense like the Dallas Cowgirls!)

This signed agreement in turn frees me from any and all of <u>his</u> stupid "disturbances." (Heretofore, "disturbances" includes interruptions while doing my nails in order to make him dinner, interrupting my sleep for his infrequent (not to mention ineffectual) attempts at love-making, or making me iron his shirts while I'm on the phone with my friends discussing the "soaps"!

Signed on this day _____ by

_____   _____
(The Wife)   (The Husband)

TERMS OF PARENT-DAUGHTER AGREEMENT

Mr. and Mrs. _____ hereby
agree to let Mr. _____ escort
their daughter _____ to the
_____ on Saturday night

ON THE CONDITION THAT:
1. He gets her home by 11:30 PM sharp.
2. Her lipstick isn't smeared.
3. Her clothes are intact and in place.
4. She returns with no strange smells on her breath.
5. There are no purplish marks on her neck.

FAILURE TO COMPLY WILL RESULT IN:
1. Her not going out for a month.
2. Her not going out with him ever again.
3. No additions to her wardrobe for two months.
4. Having to clean her own room.

ONE-WAY CONTRACT BETWEEN DENTIST AND PATIENT

INASMUCH as I am necessary to the patient's health,
INASMUCH as the patient isn't necessary to my health,
INASMUCH as this attitude can best be described as "They need me more than I need them!"
THEN I, _____, D.D.S. feel free, indifferent, and independent enough to enter this self-serving, one-way contract with _____

(patient)

PROVIDING SAID PATIENT:

1. Comes for a check up every six months so that I can double my annual income.
2. Doesn't eat smelly food prior to their visit.
3. Doesn't lie when I ask how often they floss.
4. Doesn't scream regardless of the pain I've induced when other patients are in the waiting room.
5. Answers all my superficial questions despite the suctions, clamps, etc. I've inserted in their mouth.
6. Doesn't expect me to stay in the room while I take their x-rays with my antiquated equipment.

_____

(patient's signature)

LEGAL CONTRACT BETWEEN CHILD AND BABYSITTER

I, _____, age ___
agree to go to bed exactly at _____ PM
with my teeth already brushed and without nonsense and stalling or otherwise driving my babysit-
ter, _____, insane

PROVIDING:

1. I can watch what TV programs I want to up to
   and including the hour specified above.
2. I can watch all the commercials shown, _and_ the
   closing credits, theme song, etc.
3. I can swap an extra half hour for not squealing
   about boyfriends who drop in, non-allotted
   snacks consumed, and phone calls exceeding
   two hours.

Agreed to this day by

_____   _____
      (BRAT)   (SITTER)

When I was a kid growing up in Brooklyn in the 40's and 50's, things were **different**! There was **respect** for cops then, they were important to the neighborhood! Officer Sweeny, for instance! He was like **part** of the **family**! He'd have **dinner** with us **every Friday night**, after carrying my father home from the **beer joint**! He'd always make us laugh, saying how my pop was "**never** in **jail** but always ended up **behind bars!**" Because of Sweeny, I always dreamed I'd be a cop when I grew up! I was the only kid on the block who payed **stickball** with a **night stick** instead of a **broom handle**!

In the 60's if you used a night stick for **anything** you got accused of "**police brutality**"! There was a big push on for "**non-violent apprehension**." We were expected to beat our adversary into submission with **words** and **understanding**...

It is your **repressed hostility**, stemming from your **childhood**, that has made you throw that man through the store window, friend! Not that your feelings are **wrong**, mind you, only that your **response** is **inappropriate**! We must not **victimize** the **innocent** for what **society** has **inflicted** on us, **must we**?

The popular music scene of the 60's was caught between a soft

R O C K

and a hard roll. Not since 1776 did a "British Invasion" have as much impact on this country as when The Beatles landed to appear on "The Ed Sullivan Show"—a guest shot heard 'round the world! Our own "revolutionaries" sang declarations of independence, freedom, lifestyles and even politics with jazz, country, western, and coastal overtones to the tune of gold records, big bucks, fast rises to the top and even faster falls to obscurity!

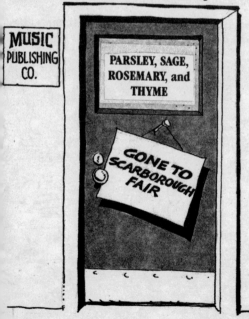

MUSIC PUBLISHING CO.

PARSLEY, SAGE, ROSEMARY, and THYME

GONE TO SCARBOROUGH FAIR

Pesticide
(Sung to the tune of "Yesterday")

Pesticide!
Spraying all that poison far and wide!
They've denied it, but we know they've lied—
'Cause they've relied on pesticide!

Naturally—
Ain't the way it's growing on a tree!
If your apple tastes like DDT—
You may not die quite naturally!

So the things they grow make us glow from deep inside
That's the price we pay when they spray with cyanide!

Pesticide!
We can't fight it 'cause our hands are tied!
Certain facts we know they'll always hide—
No prophets guide when profits ride!

They con "con" to "pro" as they snow the countryside!
Though the price we pay for their spray is genocide!

Brain Docs Keep Workin' On My Head
(Sung to the tune of "Raindrops Keep Fallin' On My Head")

Brain docs keep workin' on my head;
'Cause shrinks know that guys like me will
    keep them all well-fed!
Eatin' up my bread!
Those brain docs are workin' on my head—
    they keep workin'
They just sit—it's like I'm talkin' to the wall!
When I say I'd rather take that bread and have a ball!
They said if I did—
Then brain docs stop workin' on my head—
    wouldn't need 'em!
'Cause that means—I was cured!
A shrink knows it's a tip-off
When you flip-off
And tell him that you realize it's one big rip off!

Brain docs keep workin' on my head;
But I'm gonna go until my mind is fin'ly dead!
Then I'll be like them!
And start makin' money from each flake I'll be fakin'!
That's what I'll do—
I'll become a shrink too!

Bridge Over Troubled Molars
(Sung to the tune of "Bridge Over Troubled Waters")

When you're aging,
Lookin' shot:
When you are hangin' low—
Change what you've got
Cosmetically!
You can substitute,
Add, cut down—just like ZAP!
Like a bridge over troubled molars
With a porcelin cap—
Like a bridge over troubled molars,
You can fill each gap!

If you're balding—
Get a wig!
A face-lift if you sag!
Is your nose big?
They'll cut it down
And they'll point it up!
So just pick up the phone—
They can add more to what came natural
With some silicone!
Simply add more to what came natural
With some silicone!

Clothes Were The Way
(Sung to the tune of "Those Were The Days")

Once a business suit meant you're in business!
Once a top-notch salesman wore a tie!
That was the time when blue jeans were for farmers!
It took a Harris Tweed to make them buy!
Clothes were the way, my friend,
To make a buyer spend;
A salesman always had to look his best!
Whether he'd win or lose
Was in the clothes he'd choose!
The best in sales was always the best-dressed!
La la la la la la—la la la la la la!
Clothes were the way—
God knows, clothes were the way!

Nowadays the fashion world is different;
Nowadays the more that show's what goes!
Open-collared shirts down to their navels—
Oh, clothes don't make the man who makes the clothes!
Styles of today—offend!
A crummy dacron blend!
Or warm-up suits—that's how they go to work!
They choose their colors blind!
Their shoes are never shined!
They look like slobs—just like my son, the jerk!
La la la la la la—la la la la la la!
Clothes of today…
Oy vey, clothes of today!

Where Has All The Power Gone
(Sun to the tune of "Where Have All The Flowers Gone?")

Where has all the power gone?
Con Ed conned me!
Where has all the wattage gone?
There's no more flow!
"All electric" is a mess;
When you sit there power-less!
There's no juice for me to use—
I'm about to blow my fuse!

Where has all the power gone?
Gas is dwindling!
Where has all the "natural" gone?
There's no more flow!
"Gas heats best" has just one catch—
There's no gas, so stash your match!
Hot water—oh, how I yearn!
Gas pains really make me burn!

Where has all the power gone?
Empty oil tanks!
Where have all those barrels gone?
There's no more flow!
Wintertime won't be a treat
Since I've relied on oil heat!
And no crude has been accrued—
Or maybe we're being screwed!

Everybody's Joggin'
(Sung to the tune of "Everybody's Talkin'")

Everybody's joggin' lately,
But they don't know what they're doin'—
Joggin' so they don't stay behind!
People gruntin', groanin'
In their new Adidas,
Runnin' so they don't fall behind!
They're all trottin' over payment,
*   avoidin' doggy doo;*
An' sweatin' up their sweat suits like pros!
Ankles twistin' an' swellin' up,
*   an' turnin' from red to blue—*
Payin' their orthopedists through the nose!
Everybody's joggin' lately,
But they don't know what they're doin'—
Some are goin' out of their mind
Tryin' to lose some fat on their behind!

The Sound of Science
(Sung to the tune of "The Sound of Silence")

Hello-progress—so, what's new?
Hello, advancement—how's by you?
Got some federal funds for trying
New electronic ways of spying!
As for cancer—it's just got to wait its turn
While we earn!
And that's—the sound of science!

Thanks to ovens microwave—
Instant meals will be the rave!
We don't care much about nutrition!
A starving world is not our mission!
There's no cash in ending hunger—so why try?
Let 'em die!
And that's—the sound of science!

He's A Big Brain But Dullsville
(Sung to the tune of "Take The Last Train To Clarkesville")

He's a big brain but Dullsville,
And although I find him boring,
He's got a rich man's potential,
And I find it hard ignoring bales of dough!
How I love dough! Dough-dough-dough-dough!
His old man is a doctor,
Who's got stacks of money piled,
Which all has to go to Junior,
'Cause he is an only child!
Should poppa go—ho ho ho ho!
So I'll mary just for love—
My love of dough!

He's a big brain but Dullsville,
He's not much for conversation,
But I've interest in the interest
From the bank accumulation
Of his dough! I watch it grow! Ho ho ho ho!
We'll be married in the springtime,
I'll be dressed just like a queen,
With my gown and veil and flowers
Dyed the money shade of green—
It's apropos!
'Cause I love dough! Ho ho ho ho!
Yes, I'm marrying the creep to get his dough!

Boat Size Now
(Sung to the tune of "Both Sides Now")

Once a sports car rated high—
A status symbol you would buy;
Despite a price range in the sky,
It was the thing to do!
But now those wheels have lost their clout,
And what was "in" you find is "out"—
The time has come, without a doubt,
To change your point of view!
They judge you by your boat size now—
From aft to fore (that's stern to bow)—
To make your image stay afloat . . .
You have to buy a bigger boat!

I recall another age
When super pads were all the rage;
Your living space the only guage
Of how your status grew!
But now whatever pad you've had
Has gone the way of every fad;
The bread you've spent—well, that's too bad;
Today there's something new!
You measure up by boat size now,
From portside aft to starboard bow;
The only way that you can gloat
Is when you have a bigger boat!

Dress yourself in fancy clothes
With labels everybody knows,
And strike a fashion model pose
Like Pucci-Gucci-Coo!
But don't feel bad if no one stares,
'Cause status ain't what someone wears;
Those days are gone and no one cares;
The "best-dressed" phase is through!
They only look at boat size now;
If your yacht's got more beam to bow;
And if you don't—you lose your vote!
You gotta have the biggest boat!

The 60's saw many changes in the eating habits of the nation as the interest in

FOOD AND WINE

went from snob appeal to mob appeal to slob appeal and back up again....

On the cold front, home freezer chests ushered in the age of frozen food. But as with most advantageous changes in lifestyle, new problems arose as well. For instance, "The Mother," programmed from youth to be responsible for a homecooked meal for her family each night, suffered pangs of guilt when complete dinners were made available to her just for the thawing...

I know why they're called "TV dinners," Doctor Pastor—I can watch TV all day instead of cooking!

I know! Have you tried the "Shrimp Scampi"? My wife serves it to me every lousy night!

But for every problem, there's a smart businessman out there waiting to make his million with a clever solution! For instance, one way for "The Mother" to leave no trace of a short cut cooking process was to market complete frozen dinners in the style of the way her family was used to eating...

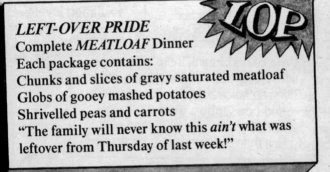

LEFT-OVER PRIDE
Complete *MEATLOAF* Dinner
Each package contains:
Chunks and slices of gravy saturated meatloaf
Globs of gooey mashed potatoes
Shrivelled peas and carrots
"The family will never know this *ain't* what was leftover from Thursday of last week!"

OVER-DONE DELIGHTS
Charred LAMB CHOP Dinner
Each package contains:
Scorched lamb chops
Burnt French fried potatoes
Over-baked beans
"Looks, smells and tastes just like the dinners you used to *over-prepare*—but *this* one takes only 8 minutes!"

Gourmets are not born, they're made. And what better time to expose a person to the joys of epicurean delights than as an infant...

To dedicated wine lovers, grapes are not fruit to be eaten, but merely wine in an immature, solid state! And this decade found many new enthusiasts who agreed with those sediments exactly. Wine is known to effect all people differently. For example, it makes some more philosophical...

...and some more realistic...

As **best man,** it is customary that I make the toast to the **bride** and **groom!** I congratulate them **especially** on their choice of this **1961 Taittinger Comtes de Champagne!** Served in magnum, it has the color of light straw gold; a complex, yeasty, but floral nose; a delicate, almost creamy texture; fruity and well-balanced flavor; and a rich, lingering palate impression! In short—**the pinnacle of elegance!**
Let's hope the **happy couple** can **say** the **same** of **one another** after **their** first **five years!**

Wine brings out the business acumen in certain individuals...

I'm thinking of selling my **La Tache '70 short** and **laying away** my **Lafite '75!**

...while others respond in a creative fashion...

I know a **white wine** would go **better** with the **dinner** I'm serving, but a **red wine** would **look better** with my **tablecloth...**

The most influential force in

TELEVISION

was the ratings game. Regardless of the intelligence, tastes, or interests of countless millions, what was logged in by counted hundreds dictated what would and wouldn't appear on the home screen...

Before you turn the dial, this network would like to remind you that we're **number one** in the **ratings** for this hour! Why take chances switching channels to a **lower rated show** when you can stay with a **winner!**

Networks lost their concern for quality when they learned that shows ranging from mediocre to garbage scored higher, and so, the "golden age of television" was buried in the vast wasteland. Every now and then, a creative, intelligent, and tasteful show like the following might pop up on the box, but if its ratings didn't soar, then it was destined to be lost in...

SPACE—the fatal frontier! There may be future voyages of the starship Yentaprise, with ongoing missions to explore strange, new worlds like full-length movies...

to seek out new life from new audiences...

to boldly go where no cancelled TV show has gone before!

Another popular trend was monster and freaky-families-at-home shows...

THE MODO FAMILY

starring Quasi Modo

and his brothers	Neo Modo
Semi Modo	Ersatz Modo
Pseudo Modo	Manny Modo,

and Esmeralda, the Dame of Notre

...and now I'd like to play a few requests!

How about, "Michelle, My Bell, Quasi dearest?

To camouflage the emphasis on high ratings with low content, networks sometimes sandwiched an "educational show" between two slices of dread, like...

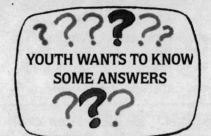

YOUTH WANTS TO KNOW SOME ANSWERS

Okay, panel, the questions we're going to tackle today are: 1) Why do salmon swim upstream to spawn? 2) How does a cactus grow without water? And 3) What effect, if any, does Bernouli's principle of flight have on today's rocketry and jet propulsion?

The only problem was that most teenagers couldn't care less about such things! If network biggies had any smarts, they'd have realized they could accomplish both—an educational show with high ratings—by concerning themselves with matters the kids were very much interested in...

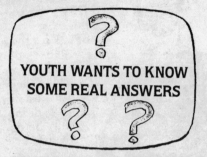

...a panel of experts who will address these questions sent in by you viewers...
• What *really* causes pimples, and how do I get rid of them without having to stop doing what may be causing them?
• Where can I find out everything I'd like to know about sex?
• Where can I go to actually *apply* this sexual knowledge once I've found out?

The search for shlock continued. Shows like "Dr. Kildare" and "Ben Casey" started an incurable rash of other medical fiascos like...

SCOTT MOGER
MEDICAL RESEARCHER

Look at it **this way,** Dr. Moger— all the **research** thus far has been collected from the **external approach!** We've been looking for causes **outside** of typical, every day human reference!

Are you suggesting we attack this virus strain from an **inside approach,** Dr. Ross, as if the strain was **internally created?**

FADS, FASHIONS, TRENDS and LOOSE ENDS

While one Spock fooled around in the world of outer space, another Spock, a doctor, fooled around in the world of "my own space." His beliefs and ideas about parenting became the standard by which millions of children were raised, thereby ushering in the trend towards permissiveness that swept the country...

KIDS COUNT, PARENTS DON'T

THEY'RE OKAY, YOU STINK

The CENTER of ANY UNIVERSE is a SON

GOD is a WOMAN—and SHE'S YOUR DAUGHTER!

GIVE YOUR CHILDREN THEIR WAY OR YOU'LL DESTROY THEM!

REASON WITH THEM UNTIL YOU LEARN TO BEND TO THEIR WISHES

That doesn't make Mommy **happy!** But if all your **toys** were **picked up,** that would make Mommy **happy!** Don't **you** want to see Mommy happy?

Yes, Mommy! If all the toys were picked up, you'd be so **happy!** And I **love** to see Mommy so happy, so I'll let **you** pick up **all the toys!**

There were many causes people aligned themselves to, and while most were for the general good and represented a step forward, there always seemed to be some reactionary force looking to halt progress if not reverse it completely...

We represent the united **"Save the Whales," "Think About Tomorrow,"** and **"Protect our Wildlife"** associations!

Oh, **yeah?** Well we're for the **"Kill 'Em All"** force—that includes your big, clumsy **whales,** your dopey **baby seals,** and your stupid **wolves!**

Women united to seek equality in a world
dominated by male chauvinist pigs! And many

politicians, aware of the voting power such a constituency could yield, responded...

I believe that **women** can play an **important role** in **government,** and I'm determined to seek out those women who are **equal** to men in intelligence and ability and **exploit** their talents! I believe a woman can add a certain **sensitivity** that is sorely lacking, and she can get **coffee** for the **guys** when **critical decisions** are being acted upon!

Student demonstrations became the **rage!** Why not, just college kids letting off a little **steam!** When I was that age we used to hear about **"panty raids,"** but that **died** in the 60's when girls **stopped wearing underwear!** So the kids go on **strike** instead, take over a few administration buildings, lock up a few professors—you know, just having a little **peace-loving fun...**

Women's hair fashion went from "bee hive" to "artichokes." They washed and conditioned hair with eggs, beer, sugar and water, and so many other "natural" ingredients that nutritionists maintained they put healthier stuff on their heads than in their stomachs. To meet the constant style changes of long hair to short hair and back to long, **wigs** became the vogue...

It was easy to start one's own religion and become "ordained" through the mail by an "order" or "sect" which, for a nominal fee, would send a certification like the following...

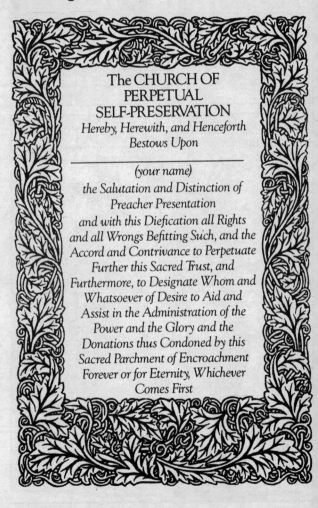

The CHURCH OF
PERPETUAL
SELF-PRESERVATION
*Hereby, Herewith, and Henceforth
Bestows Upon*

_____

(your name)
*the Salutation and Distinction of
Preacher Presentation
and with this Diefication all Rights
and all Wrongs Befitting Such, and the
Accord and Contrivance to Perpetuate
Further this Sacred Trust, and
Furthermore, to Designate Whom and
Whatsoever of Desire to Aid and
Assist in the Administration of the
Power and the Glory and the
Donations thus Condoned by this
Sacred Parchment of Encroachment
Forever or for Eternity, Whichever
Comes First*

Not all "prophets" were self-appointed, however. "Gurus" took many shapes and forms, depending upon the trend or the need, and analysts, therapists, etc. began to saturate the scene...

Tell me about it! Hey, I went to a **shrink** myself in the 60's! I wouldn't kid you! I was all **confused**— the public, for whom we risked our lives to protect, **resented us,** and it seemed like the charge of **"police brutality"** was **worse** than any **crime** some bum could commit! So I figured maybe a shrink could help me feel better...

I told him all this at my **first sessions!** He says, "I can see why you'd be **having problems!** It would be natural with so many **ill feelings** directed to policemen today! Why don't you lie down on the couch and make yourself comfortable, **PIG!**"

That from a guy who's charging me **35 bucks** an hour to make me **feel better!** In those days **35 bucks** was **25 bucks** and an **hour** was **50 minutes!** I told him, "Hey, I'm an **honest** cop, I don't make that much! How long is this treatment going to take?" He says, could you afford **3 sessions** a week if I though it was **necessary?**" I said, "Would you think it was **necessary** if I **couldn't** afford it?" He says, "You're **cured!** Get outta here!"

Then I heard about a **free** shrink program they started for **cops,** so I applied! Why not? What did I have to lose, my **mind?** I knew I didn't have much of **that** when I decided to **join** the **force!** Hah! This operation was very **different**—strictly **no frills!** The **"office"** was whichever **cell** in the back of the precinct was **empty** at the time, the **"couch"** was a **wooden bench,** and the **shrink** was a retired **interogation officer** who got his **"diploma"** from a **mail correspondence course!**

He'd shine this light in my eyes and **fire questions** at me! But I wouldn't **break!** The guys locked up in the other cells could **hear** all this and they'd yell, "Don't be a **fink**! Don't tell the creep **nothin'**! **Plead** the 5th!"

I finally told this nut job I was getting more problems from therapy than I had when I first started it! He said, "The public appears to rebel against authority, but actually it's really seeking out strength and leadership! You've got to exercise your male figure head in society!" I said, "Are you kidding? I lock up guys for doing things like that! I'm beginning to think some of you shrinks are more fraud than Freud!" He said the same thing the first guy said, "Get outta here—you're cured!"